Slow Scrape

Gwi cuumillatstun. Uswillranka kingumni.

(Translation by the late Nick Alokli, the late Sophie
Katelnikoff Shepherd, and Florence Pestrikoff.)

TANYA LUKIN LINKLATER'S performances, works for camera, installations, and writings centre Indigenous peoples' lived experiences, (home)lands, and structures of sustenance. Her performances in relation to objects in exhibition, scores, and Ancestral belongings generate what she has come to call felt structures. Her work has been shown at the Aichi Triennale, Art Gallery of Ontario, Chicago Architecture Biennial, New Museum Triennial, San Francisco Museum of Modern Art, Toronto Biennial of Art, and elsewhere. In 2021 she received the Herb Alpert Award in the Arts. Her Alutiiq/Sugpiaq homelands are in the Kodiak Island archipelago in southwestern Alaska.

Tanya Lukin Linklater

Slow Scrape

Talonbooks

Second Edition: 2022

Talonbooks
9259 Shaughnessy Street, Vancouver, British Columbia, Canada V6P 6R4
talonbooks.com

Talonbooks is located on xʷməθkʷəy̓əm, Sḵwx̱wú7mesh, and səlilwətaʔɬ Lands.

First printing: 2022

Typeset in Bely and Scala Sans
Printed and bound in Canada on 100% post-consumer recycled paper

Cover design by Typesmith. Interior design by LOKI
Cover photograph by Liz Lott from *The treaty is in the body* (2017)

Talonbooks acknowledges the financial support of the Canada Council for the Arts, the Government of Canada through the Canada Book Fund, and the Province of British Columbia through the British Columbia Arts Council and the Book Publishing Tax Credit.

Library and Archives Canada Cataloguing in Publication

Title: Slow scrape : poems / Tanya Lukin Linklater.
Names: Lukin Linklater, Tanya, author.
Identifiers: Canadiana 2022041162X | ISBN 9781772015249 (softcover)
Subjects: LCGFT: Poetry.
Classification: LCC PS8623.U514 S56 2022 | DDC C811/.6—dc23

Introduction

by Layli Long Soldier

Before entering *Slow Scrape*, I knew something about Tanya Lukin Linklater, which I cannot help but celebrate: she is an artist who is not confined to writing, but when her work does arrive to the container of a page, it radiates an undeniable life force of *possibility*. Lukin Linklater works in performance, choreography, video, sculpture, poetry, and non-fiction; this work is often site specific. Throughout these various modes, she is ever and always a community collaborator and a disciplined thinker. Upon receiving the K.M. Hunter Award for Literature, she explained, "Often I work in performance using written scores for movement as ways to locate choreography. The score is a visual, spatial, textual space between the dancer and I. This finding of a dance later may be translated to the form of the video." In this, I can appreciate a creative circuitry in Lukin Linklater's writing – beginning with the purity of language, that guides another process, which then leads to an alternate, yet fully developed form. I sense from this collection of texts, however, that this creative process is not always linear, but simultaneous. Movement, as she has explained, is often concurrent to her text. Therefore, when I am enlivened by the language and subject matter, I am just as "moved" by Lukin Linklater's *way* of working, her *way* of thinking, and *way* of making. It is uniquely hers, permeated with unmistakable intellectual and creative sovereignty.

Given this, we can also appreciate the way in which *Slow Scrape* is neither wholly poem nor verbose prose and exposition, but reads as text in step – toe-to-floor, light and gentle or heel-to-earth, pounding; felt from ground, up. That is to say, this work is most understood in how it lands along notes. Central to Lukin Linklater's work is *score* and *notation*, wherein, traditionally speaking, symbols or marks represent elements of music; indicate instructions; or serve as shorthand commentary and observation. Only here, symbols of notation are found in the symbols of word choice and particular terms. For example, in the short piece, "Suk," Lukin Linklater writes, "*Suk* / A human being. Afognak dialect: the S is pronounced SH. It sounds like shook but with a shorter o. Perhaps we shake. Or past tense, we shook. When are we shaken?" The term *Suk* is symbol for something greater, and in this case, becomes the Greater Question: *When are we (us, human beings) shaken?* Our answers surely vary, though surely, in asking we feel beneath us a "seismic undulation ... no longer a tremble but a roll a roar a boom that does not end."

Along the same lines, Lukin Linklater is determinedly precise in the lexicon she employs. As we think about *symbol* – its representation of the bigger or greater – we see how the word choices of "Alutiiq," "Afognak," "Nipissing First Nation," "The Crow Fair," or "Astisak" not only anchor the work in respectful, cultural specificity, but are also the signposts – markers, if you will – for larger issues and structures set before us in this book. Lukin Linklater writes, "An Alutiiq person enters and says / We exceed the discipline formation of Anthropology. / Then / We exceed the structures imposed on us." We can understand how "Alutiiq" in this piece, for example, serves a greater intent. Here, Lukin Linklater refuses generalities – forgoing commonly accepted terms such as "Native American" or "Indigenous." This refusal (or resistance) is, simply put, a fierce refusal of *erasure* – this insidious force sweeping us, globally, at landslide pace towards a devastating and unimaginable future.

Yet, what we encounter in Lukin Linklater's writing is not typical to many works of political and social "resistance," because her approach is built on a thesis of power – and this power is not established through dominance nor simplistic defiance; rather it is cultivated from *relation(ship)*. Through particulars of place, language, and culture, people begin to know each other; and erasure (rife with overlooking, forgetting, denial and invisibility) becomes impossible. When Lukin Linklater writes, "An Alutiiq person enters and says / Our memory marks Afognak. / Afognak marks us. / What are we tethered to? What holds us together?," she asks us to consider what binds, what connects human relationships by centring, first, the land; where we come from establishes who we are to one another. It's in this relationship, then, that we are able to feel the impact of her words, "When I am home on our island I sense that the land exudes grief. / Many of us have left the land of our Ancestors / perhaps because the grief becomes unbearable." At moments like this, I begin to think about what awakens, shatters, or leaves us raw in literature. Out of the unbearable and seemingly unspeakable, ground is broken. We *feel* for one another. The soil of the spirit is plowed. And true empathy, meaningful action, and change can begin.

Another aspect of Lukin Linklater's work that should not be overlooked is her high regard for women – within family and community, among those who embody memory, story, and cultural knowledge; as well women in positions of leadership, fellow artists, and intellectuals. Throughout Lukin Linklater's career, she has collaborated with women and one could view these working relationships casually, attributing them to natural gravitation or connection. However, I propose that Lukin Linklater is intentional in her decision making. Throughout *Slow Scrape*, women are referenced: her mother, her Nohkom, Malala Yousafzai, Chief Theresa Spence, Leanne Betasamosake Simpson, Maria Tallchief, Mary Anne Barkhouse, and more. The long poem "The Harvest Sturdies" is an incredible example of Lukin Linklater's traverse into the leadership, wisdom, knowledge, and artistry of women, beginning with the galvanizing hunger strike of Attawapiskat's Chief Theresa Spence in 2012 and 2013. Then the poem unfolds into an epic, ingenious union of both visual and documentary poetics (the likes of which I have not before seen) using interviews with family members about the Cree process for making James Bay mitts. One whole page of the poem, for instance, is dedicated solely to two lines: "mitts : astisak / women : iskwewak." Moments like these are important moves and contributions to contemporary literature as this generation of Native artists and scholars faces a terrifying history of, again, *erasure* – that is, an undeniable absence of Native women's perspectives from historical documentation. We reckon with countless books produced by anthropologists and non-Native writers who have woven their way into Tribal communities. For the most part, these visitors are/were men and, most often, collected information, stories, and accounts from, likewise, other men. What has resulted is a lopsided, unjustly incomplete written record of knowledge in our Tribal communities – women's contributions are frequently missing, entirely. Yet many are working to build a newer, balanced knowledge base. Addressing her Nohkom (grandmother), Lukin Linklater writes, "Now as we talk on the phone, you in Peawanuck me on Lake Nipissing, I wonder why I never asked you more. I waited so long." Yet the shining importance here is, Lukin Linklater has asked.

I am compelled to return to the choreography in Lukin Linklater's other creative endeavours, because inherent to the role of choreographer is leadership, connection, reciprocity, and a flow that allows some amount of improvisation. These qualities, likewise, shape *Slow Scrape*. There is a steady hand in Lukin Linklater's writing – at times, the text is built through direct statement. At times, textured by poiesis that loosens the imagination. But what's most meaningful is, as a reader, I am allowed to take leaps, I am allowed to think for myself. Lukin Linklater directs without submitting to explanation. In this expansive and undulating meditation on time, relations, origin, and colonization, Lukin Linklater guides and leads, all the while allowing us freedom to participate. When she writes, "Spend time with the work. Be generous. / Generous–ness as potentiality, as a becoming," I listen. I will follow the score. With her, I am becoming.

—Layli Long Soldier

Slow Scrape

SLOW SCRAPE

One then another

a yielding record
a record cultivated
so it will be held

to scrawl and carve, crowd then hew

I place one then another
until the gap between is less and we know
something together

Not Like Us

because   breath crackles, I angle to light   a cadenced tread

We hide in the spruce trees our tiny bodies in branches above a black sand beach. Peeking out at the dark water, no coats. No luggage. Mustard-coloured float plane, propeller roaring then resting. A white man with a yellow beard: "Travelling light?" I don't remember seeing my mother, but I imagine her there with red feathered hair and white polyester pants like in the family photo Dad keeps today.

And this is how I remember it, I sit on the floor with my sisters, Mom in a chair tells the lady until her face crumples, blotches. For a while, two girl cousins live below us. Their dad stays with them, not like us. Not like us, their blonde hair and Barbie Dream House. My sisters and I, we play house in the metal legs of a grey ironing board.

My crossna, he sends $100 for my fifth birthday. Mother, we need to hook up the power and cable and phone and buy food, I see the groceries pile by the cashier. She asks for a carton of Camel's. Later I watch her talk and talk while Billy Idol sings "White Wedding" on MTV, she smokes.

Dad knuckles a borrowed Buick down a slick, black road past the hospital. Sisters and I in the front share one seatbelt. The heavy side door lurches open. Sarah is nearest the door, she is the smallest. He reaches over us and slams the door shut, still driving. The last time I see him he gives us brand new pink coats. The twins' coats match.

I tell sisters that my baby doll will be safest in the box that holds all of the important papers. We play with Mom's hair as she stares down the highway, her eyes bloodshot. She sleeps in the front seat of the tiny Chevette, we watch huskies eat their own vomit through the car windows. When we arrive the one box that is missing from the moving truck has all of the important papers in it.

in this   incremental comfort   in notation   I remember   re-

                                                                          notation

This is my childhood unmade and made, the oldest of three girls, hold hands skip stones catch minnows swim naked cool creeks salt lagoon. We fly away from our home village

to women's resource centre that low income housing Kodiak, ocean on all sides my relatives in Aleutian Homes thick smell of canneries near tent city, I am five.

The twins are four, suck their thumbs. I pour them cereal, we stand on chairs against the sink. Rain falls on spruce needles branches sap rain falls on hands hair lips. Kindergarten:

we eat ants on a log, a bathroom stall sits in class, we sleep on mats. I chase a blonde girl she laughs skips jumps slides away. Halloween: teacher dresses me in a cape and lipstick

for the school parade. Later sisters and I find long skirts quilted jackets, we mimic Roma, we duck from wind in doorways for treats in Aleutian Homes. Outside

Alaska strangers look at our straight dark hair our white mother, they're confused by our hair she says they think we're Black. They ask if we are triplets, the twins wear

matching yellow dresses fluttery polka dots white ankle socks straight bangs smiles in polaroids Easter Bunny, my dress hangs off-colour. Each time a stranger asks, I wish

we were triplets but they're twins. I get terribly thin, smell of cannery and rain blue tarp tents the ocean on all sides, I'm made and unmade in Polaroids, I slip away

from school. I look for her at the college, my mother among spruce trees smell of wet ground rough brown brick on my fingertips, what is this place she comes to, away

from us? I change into panties a child-sized bra, in class we slide jump grapevine to music, I see the women smile their kind eyes in mirrors as my mother and I dance. 1982.

then

as mourning dove s wing s   whistle   my footfall startle s andthe pattern upend s

·her shifts sleeps she nursing home she $3.00 hour her shifts then deputy sheriff her her sleep sleep she uniforms she white shoes she shifts she black boots and uniform I I I look her bedroom her sleeps me pass she bedroom I school she gone gone we home her gone her sleep we get gone she $3.00 me sleep I school I home we cheese blocks them heavy cans them labels them black white them letters and cheese blocks I throat me cheese throat me stick we labels she $3.00 she food stamps them brown and red them bright we play money she black boots she uniform her sleep sleep we look she

A Colorado valley, the western slope of the Rocky Mountains, I am eight. Third grade we move to Texas Avenue then Belford Avenue then Gunnison Avenue, pack unpack repack

around Grand Junction my sisters and I scattered. We share a bunk bed, a willow tree rains worm bugs. They seep in to crevices of the house burrow into the bedroom squirm

on the bunk bed while we sleep we flick their striped gray green black bodies but more fall. I test for the gifted program at my third school on a Saturday. The woman with wavy

brown hair and pale skin asks me questions, I write in test booklets alone, vastness of an empty classroom. This is my childhood unmade and made. She reports in a voice meant

to soothe, you missed the cut-off by one point. A sunny afternoon, my mom smokes a Camel on the concrete step outside the kitchen, dank smelling of grease. A thin man,

her tears, the Chevette. I watch them as if they're on the other side of panes of glass. We don't get another car for two years. On the other side of voices meant to soothe empty

classrooms squirming bunk beds scattered failed tests or Chevettes, on the other side of mountains bunk beds avenues my childhood was a girl, her nightly flicking at the pane.

so to re-pattern   the s low s crape   of time I do thi s-so   as to   re-traverse-it

We live with Mommy Cross those months, weed the garden for hours
in the long summer sun, catch crawdads in the irrigation ditch, spread
manure with our bare feet.

Spaghetti westerns fill the musty living room. Sometimes, for no
reason, she pinches us. Mom tells me that when I was a toddler I
pinched my baby sisters for no reason too, other times I asked why I
wasn't born a twin.

At dinner Mommy Cross calls out [   ] my cheeks, brown from the
sun, blush underneath. She keeps old tissues in her sleeves and I hear
the adults whisper senile, all while canning green beans. I grow to hate
her tomatoes.

Measurements: 1 pat of margarine per piece of toast; 1 level teaspoon
of sugar per bowl of plain Cheerios or Cornflakes; 2 teaspoons of
Tang per cup of water; 3 squares of toilet paper folded in half to clean
our waste.

  s

now s now underbrush boot s when I angle to light, breath   crackle s

Mom shifts in a nursing home three dollars an hour then she's a sheriff's deputy I look in
on her as she sleeps, I pass by the bedroom before school she's gone when we get home
gone when we fall asleep blocks of cheese and heavy cans with black-and-white
labels the cheese sticks at my throat I pretend to look
at tabloids she pulls out colourful bills like play
money one winter Santa delivers an unwrapped
cardboard box that smells faintly of cantaloupe, stuffed
bell-bottomedcorduroyfadeddenimusedshirts
1988 the girls all wear white Keds the girls wrap their textbooks
in carefully cut shopping bags precise folds that tell me
BananaRepublicUnitedColorsofBenetton 1988
stepdad crouched with bad back corners me in the kitchen
spittle tinged chew moustache he roars close roars my face
the house is his yellowed lower teeth
stubble on his dimpled chin I've never seen him work
he cracks my 1988 quiet
against the counter I watch a news program
trickle-down theory Reaganomics I'm thirteen
I know nothing
trickles down
not through
cracked counters not
through boxes
not for three dollars
not in
cans not
to us
not
to
1988
me.

Nohkom

Her hands that cradle caribou hide, sinew, all
manner of beads, fur – my hands crouch inside
the space she presses between her fingers, inside
the space resting at her palms.

Do you remember when you asked me to be your
grandmother?

I bend at the waist, wrap my arms around her
shoulders, resting against the wheelchair,

Yes, my sound to her ear.

A girl

Fair trade organic dark roast in the Bodum, I ignore
newspapers strewn across the kitchen table and CBC News
on TV to scan the Twitter feed on my iPhone, I prefer it this
way. I choose which headlines to click. Tucked into my
back pocket, the news pulses and waves, doesn't touch me.

But this morning I click on a National Post headline.
Boarding a school bus, insurgents ask for her by name, her
name means "grief stricken." I crack my wrist, thumb down
the screen. She tells a regime she will become educated.
They shoot Grief Stricken in the head and neck.

I cry. I don't know how
this can be a poem.

44 days

At twenty-one days, on the eve of the new year on unmelted river, I watch until night, fearful of what might come. Forty-four days. She relents, stays with us. She is not spent, she continues. Now that number and she know one another.

The Harvest Sturdies

cheap memory foam cushions a cheaper mattress, under goose down comforter and flannel I'm wrapped composing before I open my eyes, there's a woman whose name means to harvest, to provide.

a crimson ribbon skirt to ground, a down coat, tanned moose hide mitts braided with yarn rest at her sides held at her neck. moose hide, smoked and tanned, collide with red and white beads. those hands pluck geese chop wood snare rabbits stoke fires lay spruce boughs for warmth, the harvest sturdies.

here, I bleach black mould lines on window frames, scrub the septic tank toilet, wash rewash bathroom countertops, he pine sols the floors, stacks rugs on deck snow. together we dust scrub bleach to prepare our home for visitors.

from a hand-me-down couch through the window, an ice-fishing hut appears driven by a truck I can't see, it hovers on a dirt road to launch onto the frozen lake. this view from our 900 square-foot home on someone else's first nation.

surrounded by blankets hanging inside raw canvas and scraped trees, spruce boughs on ground to insulate, she rests. a woodstove pipe creaks towards december sun. the girls crouch on unthawed land near a fire, she sits mantled in blankets against wintry damp.

she listens as they speak about a day when every child in canada feels they are worth something. I watch as she brings her lips to each cheek and brow and I plot a line for her as these james bay mitts rest at her neck. to harvest provide dispense, she enters her twenty-first day.

the eve of a new year on the unmelted river.

mitts : astisak

women : iskwewak

James Bay astisak worked by women's hands astisak. And from the life of an animal, you say it's a year to fix a moose hide or longer, your hands

clip

scrape

smoke

wring

tan

stretch

wash

Your hands work hides beads fur linings. Stitches thread cloth. Both your hands work these objects that aren't *objects:* astisak warm the hands of awasisak   napewak iskwewak   on this land, astisak. Women who work in this way, mothers grandmothers aunties, I'm telling you. I don't know this work. Nimbly, James Bay iskwewak craft astisak. Swiftly, they sew astisak. Astisak, in repetition they stitch, swift repetition, they clothe their families.

Nohkom I call you. Ask about sewing mitts, instead you tell me you grew up in a tipi, on the land. In the bush near Hudson Bay 95, 200 miles from Peawanuck. Your dad hunted caribou, trapped beaver otter mink and nowadays the young men trap martens.

Years ago in my mother-in-law's kitchen you fried caribou with onions, ruddy on a spring afternoon in Timmins. After tea and visits in your daughter's house I told you my grandmother passed away, I was only seven. *I can be your grandmother* you said.

Now as we talk on the phone, you in Peawanuck me on Lake Nipissing, I wonder why I never asked you more. I waited so long. Nearly eighty this May and you can't cook in the tipi nor teach the kids how to snare or to speak Cree. But you sew fierce and scrub the floors from your wheelchair.

*I never saw my own mother sew stitch cook. Ghoulash canned corn dropped in macaroni second-day. Grandmother, it was a wooden red-handled rolling pin tiny bread tins the feel of dough flattened on my palms. Girl fingers, just play. Who, among women, showed me. How to [   ] small **objects** in seventh-grade Home Ec. How to [   ] a blue frock for performance [   ] beads on a silver skirt [   ] a patch. Among women, I tape the hem on slacks for an interview, sewing machine untouched.*

"

They need

to   understand   the

whole

concept

of   our

craftsmen.

"

Auntie

So it's done like this, Tanya:

seam thread needle hem seam thread needle hem seam thread needle hem seam thread

oo:::|| astisak ||:::oooo:::|| maskasina ||:::oo

seam thread needle hem seam thread needle hem seam thread needle hem seam thread

oo:::|| petal leaf stem ||:::oooo:::|| yellow purple green ||:::oo

oo:::|| daughter & son & daughter ||:::oo

oo:::|| petal leaf stem ||:::oooo:::|| yellow purple green ||:::oo

seam thread needle hem seam thread needle hem seam thread needle hem seam thread

oo:::|| astisak ||:::oooo:::|| maskasina ||:::oo

seam thread needle hem seam thread needle hem seam thread needle hem seam thread

Instead, with accent hues of moss
and lavender shades of rose, I follow
a map of syllabics

I write on ‖ a t i k o w a y a n ‖

and build my lines like this

nohkominanak

‖:::oooo:::‖ ‖:::oooo:::‖

iskwewak iskwewak iskwewak

‖:::oooo:::‖ ‖:::oooo:::‖ ‖:::oooo:::‖ ‖:::ooo:::‖

askiy askiy askiy askiy askiy askiy askiy askiy askiy askiy

‖:::oooo:::‖ ‖:::oooo:::‖ ‖:::oooo:::‖ ‖:::oooo:::‖ ‖:::oooo:::‖ ‖:::oooo:::‖

"

When it's
my own time

my   own   sewing
my   own   ways

it's like I go into a little
place of my own.

"

Auntie

practice practice practice practice practice practice practice practice practice practice
:..
a stitch a bead another stitch repeat a stitch a bead another stitch repeat a stitch a bead ano
other stitch repeat a bead a stitch another stitch repeat a stitch a bead another stitch repeat

o-o-o-o-o-o-o-o-o-o-o-o-o-o-o-o-o-o-o-o-o-o-o-o-o-o-o-o-o-o-o-o-o-o-o-o-o-o-o-o-o-o-o-o-o

hands deft every stitch straight each bead nimble repeat hands deft every stitch straight
each bead nimble repeat hands deft every stitch straight each bead nimble repeat hands de
:..
gentle   gentle   very gentle   repeat   gentle gentle   very gentle   repeat   gentle gentle   very

"

You connect with your loved ones. For me I connect with my mom it's my mom

and grandma mostly my mom though and my aunties. I have their patterns

their mitts their slippers. I pull them out I look at them. I see her writing I can

see the style of my aunts I can see the style of my mom and these papers

are little whittled now they're just thinning out. You start thinking

about them it's healing it brings real comfort in your soul

when you're sewing I get a lot of comfort. That's why

when things go on *ah I'm goin' to do some*

sewing I go in another world it's hard

to explain just with you and God

you're thinking you're praying

your mind goes you're

in another

atmosphere

"

"

I don't let it   go.   I won't let it

go.

"

smoke of the canvas skirt you bind on

a t i k o w a y a n in the cook tipi eddies

we spark the spongy wood

for this last part you show me

over the phone, Nohkom

raising one delica bead

from the cache, I fire the caribou broom

turn it over in my mind

as I cannot see its texture

weight colour, the light

You say, only three or four left

in Peawanuck and perhaps two in Fort Severn know

how to *fix* the   hide   of   a t i k

Nohkom, I am not with you

Event Score for Writing on Indigenous Contemporary Art (Mary Anne Barkhouse) 1–3

1 minute and 49 seconds: the length of the video documentation taken on an iPhone of Mary Anne Barkhouse's works, *Midden (Au Grand Couvert)*, porcelain, black clay, silk, pine, bronze, 2018–ongoing, and *Untitled I-VIII* from *The Quick and the Dead*, anthotypes and cyanotypes, 2018–ongoing.

Develop a daily practice of reading this documentation of objects, space, light, and the way in which the work calls you to move. Around the table. Longing to touch the porcelain infant turtles and broken crow-raven.

Wait to write.

Instruct yourself to write daily for 1 minute and 49 seconds, the length of the video documentation taken on an iPhone of Mary Anne Barkhouse's works.

Yearn to speak to Mary Anne Barkhouse.

Wonder about her work.

Wait to write.

Read "The Best Medicine for My Climate Grief" by Peter Kalmus and wonder if the melancholy of climate grief cancels or negates writing about Indigenous contemporary art. Or making art for that matter.

Spend time with the work. Be generous.

Generous-ness as potentiality, as a becoming.

Visiting

Mary Anne Barkhouse, first I yearn to visit with you. And then we are in relation. I listen. You tell me about the land you live with – in cottage country not far from Barrie – your travels from Turtle Island to France intheplacesnotbuiltupthatarestillwild, your grandfather's experience in Kwakiutl water with a wolf. I know the story in its short form as I have listened to documentation of you telling the story elsewhere. I wonder about the parts you leave out. About the long summers at home on the water fishing. About the way we know a place over time. The way our Ancestors have known our places over deep time. But we all keep some parts of stories for ourselves. I tell you about the water that surrounds my village in Alaska and my father. We talk at length about fishing, oil spills, and then the sun. The sun is what I remember the most. And the time that it takes to know a place. The time that it takes to know. In our bodies. In relation.

For Mary Anne Barkhouse and Sonya Kelliher-Combs

listening   and   then   t e l l i n g

    listening   then   being   with   one another   our relatives

deep time   fish camp time   city time   glacial time

    the   timeittakes   to   be

                                        in relation

Event score for this work of Mary Anne Barkhouse

Remember your visit to the gallery. The way that you tilted towards and away. The way that the light felt. The way that the light knit the table and that wall of colour (you cannot forget) together. The way that the light made a together-ness with breath.

Remember your motion around the table, the legs that carried you near the legs of the table and your longing to touch the small bits, the garbage that had been re-worked, re-made, and placed.

Remember the coy-wolf. In real life he would pace and circle, catching glimpses of your whereabouts as you walked through the city streets of Toronto or Chicago or in the bush of Algonquin Park and you would never see him. You would never experience him except when hair on the back of your neck rises, alert to his motion.

So soak him in, in this place, where his movement – crouching and skulking – has been paused. He is still yet ready, observing the table that has been set with trash and life and trash.

Feel his movement and yours. Feel his stillness and yours. His hybridity and constant motion, perhaps they make him a survivor.

Remember the feeling of motion in the installation, the death of a raven, the exploded bits of garbage, the raven-crows who are in mid-squawk, mid-call, mid-language.

Event score for a future we may never know

Remember the view of that which is unsustainable, that which cannot continue, lest we be met with deep grief.

On tables

What table are we setting for ourselves.

For midden found by Mary Anne Barkhouse near her home on the side of the road and cast in porcelain by her hands

midden, noun.

1. a. A dunghill, a dung heap, a refuse heap. Also: a domestic ash-pit.

    b. A receptacle for refuse, a dustbin; (also) an enclosure in a backyard or basement for holding dustbins or domestic refuse.

2. (excerpts) In 1827, "If there was an object on earth which Monkshaugh loathed ... it was a slatternly dirty woman ... 'What's to be done with that rampallion midden, 'Lizbeth?' said he."

    In 1859, "That everlasting midden which men call the world."

3. a. *Archaeology*. A prehistoric refuse heap which marks an ancient settlement, consisting chiefly of shells and bones and often also discarded artefacts;

    b. *Zoology* and *Palaeontology*. A heap of excreta, food remains, or other organic debris left by an animal; *esp.* such a deposit composed largely of, or cemented by, the urine of small mammals such as pack rats ...

One day if anyone survives the climate apocalypse that is upon us, anthropologists may look through our garbage made into midden for study. They will examine these bits to understand us and perhaps also why we likely disappeared.

As Leanne Betasamosake Simpson has said elsewhere we have experienced the apocalypse already and by *we* she means the Anishnaabeg. She writes from, to, and for the Anishnaabeg.

In Alaska, my home, the forces of illness, enslavement, and deep grief were shocks that repeated across generations, nestled within the seismic convulsions of Russian and American colonization. This disturbance, this distortion, has been called the Great Death.

Mary Anne Barkhouse and I visited about bison, beavers, and wolves on Turtle Island. How they were killed for bone, for fur, and for nuisance. And the devastation that ensued. Some of us have endured. Some of us have survived.

Perhaps in a future we may never know like coy-wolves or crow-ravens, bison or beaver some of us will survive. But perhaps the colonizers, who have not yet survived an apocalypse, whose history or memory have not endured, perhaps someone needs to tell them that the Great Death is upon us.

Our mother is not a midden.

In Memoriam/Unspoken–ness

Part 1

in a place where words do not exist

         no – words   pass   through my t r u n k

              d i s s o l v e

                 s i l e n c e

      five hundred   I call   by tender names

guts caught in their throats – gasping
and grasping, they fall,

      heaped   into   earth

      s u p p l e   s i l e n c e

      five hundred nestled within
          knife-sharp slate and *amiq* of sea otter
               salt spray and canon ash
                   relentless swell and musket strike

in no – place, soundlessness   passes through my   limbs lips belly

                   until tips of fingers, outline of spine   surrender to

        a parcel   heaped   with five hundred tender shoots   pulled

apart

      edges of   r e f u g e   r o c k

s o a k e d i n   u n s p o k e n – n e s s

Part 2

elltuwaq,

    ellpeklluku

        niicugniluku   *tangerlluku*

                tengluni

I hear the sound a long way off

            s c a t t e r – e d

I can't say: I know the sound or what it is meant to be

                at first   just the sensation

gentle

I   reach   with my ear

                she whispers

            she calls

        calls

    elltuwaq

until I re – call a voice, a language I do not know

heaped on this patch of language – less land

    until I hear a voice pierce static

    ellpeklluku

water laps relentless at stones

    I sip   –

        then gulp

           tongue to salt-ether

              nose to damp black earth

    niicugniluku

    I hear wings   before a call

my neckbone extends   –   to see a path above
as I remember bird silhouette
the sound of a voice rains
vibration

a thousand wings
five hundred birds

above jagged moss-encapsulated slate rock

sets   sets   sets   sets   sets

sets   sets   sets   sets   sets   *s w e l l*
sets   sets   sets   sets   sets

n e c k

sets   *bone*   sets   sets   sets   sets   sets

r o c k

sets   sets   sets   sets   sets   sets

g u t

sets   sets   sets   *a m i q*   sets   *s e t s*   *s e t s*

sets   *s e t s*   *s e t s*   *s   e   t   s*

tangerlluku

water swells, crushing rock

she calls and in this calling,

she catches the throat

she hooks the gut, relentless

tengluni

How do we traverse the slow scrape of time?

Decommission

Three men stand facing an open U-Haul. The carcass of our Jeep tucked inside is a thousand pounds. His black boots mark the white ground. At his back, a wind carves deep water.

For four years, Phil has tended to the Jeep. Sometimes it is driven ten minutes down the dirt road to his garage. Other times it is towed, billowing white smoke, to wait its turn for repair. Together, we listen to the hum grow more deafening, feel the catch cough and sputter.

Phil and his garage sit squarely on Nipissing First Nation. We live down the road in a small house. Daily we pass his house, drive to town, and for four years the Jeep has carried us across the invisible boundary between Nipissing First Nation and the City of North Bay.

He tells Phil his idea, and for a year Phil listens; he doesn't say much. He calls in town to find someone to tear the blue down to its frame, but it isn't right. Each man he speaks to makes him think of Phil and wait for his decision. He waits.

Two summers ago, we drove ten hours, thousands of kilometres south, in the refuge of the cool Jeep to the unforgivable stickiness of upstate New York. He told someone in that place of compost and art and heat and dorms that the Jeep was his horse.

I see the Crow Fair, Montana. When we were young, we camped in the tall grass. He braided my hair while Crow boys rode horses through camp, with reins but no blankets. The 10 a.m. parade each day called me. Horses in stitched beadwork. Exquisite. Shiny trucks with Elders and families in the back; truck beds wore Pendleton blankets, hoods were adorned in beads. A procession.

I see the time I traversed mountain ranges and plains, whisking three children to Oregon. How cheap the gas was how Oregon beaches interrupted how the Columbia River how tulips.

There are other stories.

When he tells me his idea, it lives in my imagination for a year or more. I turn a sculpture over in my mind, an object transforms from the utilitarian to the non-useful; quotidian to non-everyday. I picture the sculpture, sandblasted.

As it is torn down in my mind's eye, as it is decommissioned in his imagination, Phil too deconstructs the Jeep, first in his head. I hold my breath. His intention is for Phil to tend to the Jeep, one final time. To tend to the ideas of object, invisible boundaries, and the time it takes to build relationships. We wait for his decision.

For four days, the Jeep is pulled apart and boiled down. For four days, Phil labors.

It sits, tucked inside the U-Haul, as a rusted carcass. I catch a glimpse and no longer remember all that I wanted to say about living with this object for six years.

My ideas about the object are not the same as the object itself. My ideas are only part of the negotiation between these men and the thousand pounds left.

Suk

A human being. Afognak dialect: the S is pronounced SH. It sounds like shook but with a shorter o. Perhaps we shake. Or past tense, we shook. When are we shaken?

An Event Score for Indigenous Epistemologies (Eber Hampton)

A person enters and reads

        The audience listens but does not look

Then

        The audience looks only to follow with its body

Then

        The audience's body turns to the east

Then

        The audience holds its heart

Then

        The audience listens but does not look

An Event Score for Haunting (Eve Tuck)

A person enters and reads

                    The audience remembers relentlessly

Then

                    The audience feels no ease

Then

                    What can decolonization mean other than the return of stolen land?

Then

                    What must it feel like to be haunted

An Event Score for Maria Tallchief, Dylan Robinson, and Sherry Farrell Racette

A person enters and says

> The museum or gallery exerts a force in its looking.

Then

> The look of a choreographer is like an everyday structure that exerts a force alongside the body of a dancer.

Then

> Our bodies exert a force.

Then

> Our objects exert a force.

Then

> When do our bodies' forces exceed the look of a choreographer?

Then

> When do our objects' forces exceed the look of the museum or gallery?

An Event Score for Kodiak Alutiit 1 (Helen Simeonoff)

An Alutiiq person enters and says

This event score is longer than most. My job is to tell. Your job is to listen. Listen to the quiet around the words. Listen for the sparse and melancholic.

Then

Alphonse Pinart collected Alutiiq masks on our island in 1872 and took them to France.

Then

Over a century later Helen Simeonoff, our relative, travelled from Kodiak Island to the masks held in a collection in France. She was the first.

Then

Many Alutiit travelled from Kodiak Island to the masks held in a collection in France. They tell us that when they touched the masks they wept.

Then

The Alutiiq masks eventually travelled back to Kodiak Island but only because we had an Alutiiq Museum to exhibit them and only if we promised to never repatriate the masks.

Then

The promise was made and vitrines were built.

Then

We looked at the masks behind glass. Some masks we quickly looked away from. Which masks were we supposed to see? Mostly we looked at the texts alongside the masks that attempted to tell us what the masks meant.

Then

We felt the masks when we looked at them.

Then

We felt the masks when we touched them.

Then

We think about the text remnants (behind glass, placed next to the masks) left by Alphonse Pinart and all that was held in our people before he ever travelled to our island to collect.

Then

We exceed the text remnants in Pinart's translations of our songs and dances from Alutiiq to Russian to English to French and back again.

Then

We exceed the Alphonse Pinart collection of Alutiiq masks.

An Event Score for Kodiak Alutiit 2 (to Aleš Hrdlička)

An Alutiiq person enters and says

        We exceed the archaeological site.

    Then

        We exceed the discipline formation of Anthropology.

    Then

        We exceed the structures imposed on us.

An Event Score for the Epistemic Violence of Translation (Edgar Heap of Birds)

1. A person enters and speaks in Alutiiq

2. A person enters and speaks in Alutiiq

    The audience listens

An Event Score for Afognak Alutiit 1–3 (Abridged)

An Alutiiq person enters and says

                  Our memory marks Afognak.

                              Afognak marks us.

What are we tethered to?   What holds us together?

    When I am home on our island I sense that the land exudes grief.

                              This feeling.

    Many of us have left the land of our Ancestors

           perhaps because the grief becomes   unbearable.

An Event Score for Afognak Alutiit 4

An Alutiiq person enters and tells a story about Afognak.

    The audience listens

        Then

            Someone tells a related story.

                And so on. And so on. And so on. And so

Suk

A human being. Afognak dialect: the S is pronounced SH. It sounds like shook but with a shorter o. Perhaps we shake. Or past tense, we shook. When are we shaken?

They fall the ground beneath you

I say this even. Perhaps you hear it resolute. Or the words jump jagged at you
they fall the ground beneath you so that you are sliding on silt down the side of
a bluff to mudflats terrified but focused on one point like the dust in the air or
a dog attached to a house on a leash that jumps with the will of land.

I tell you that in places the ground becomes a mouth. Roofing tiles gypsum screws
curtains glass stainless steel mixing bowls tufts of carpet kneaded with rock silt
snow pussywillows. Houses unmade. A little girl sits on a car with her brother.
A slide a shift a shove. Jagged earth under current pulls to tide. They land.
Even, still and quiet. Her oldest and smallest brothers do not land. They become
landed. The debris is eaten by the tides.

What happens when the earth shocks convulses jars, when a seismic undulation
is no longer a tremble but a roll a roar a boom that does not end?
One long percussive wreck.
Accelerating but you do not know   what speed   or where   or when   it will halt.

You see the fissure rift schism splinter. What are these words tethered to? As the breach
fragments. What holds them together? All this silt sedimenting   powder settling.

What are we tethered to when everything seems to   collapse   shatter   erupt
    simultaneously?

Afognak was destroyed by tsunamis. I say it for what it is. The weight of the words
rolls in the empty spaces of my mouth. What are these words tethered to?

My great uncle JP *The earthquake first and the water started moving.*

My uncle Allen tells me that my grandfather Afonie Jr. was in his boat travelling back from Kodiak when the earth shook. My aunts and uncles, small, were playing on the beach.

Betty Nelson *The ground was just going in waves. I remember stepping over these waves even on the on the ground. And underneath your feet it sounded like a freight train you know going passing by or something. It was terrible noise.*

She describes the eery snowfall when the land halted.

Victoria Nelson Woodward describes the erratic flying of birds. Not a murmuration.

Zenida ran across Big Lake with Maria, three years old, on her back.
As Zenida and her six children ran across the lake the ice broke up behind them.
The ones they speak of, my grandmother aunties uncles my father my relatives.

The people ran to the mountain.

My dad remembers that when the people arrived on the mountain wall tents sheltered the people. The people stayed on the mountain for two nights. On the third day they walked back down to the village.

The creeks and lake had turned to saltwater. Driftwood amongst spruce trees.
The community hall just complete broken up. The water high in the houses.

The land that was marked with square log cabins and sod homes banyas chicken
coops gardens smokehouses boats nets firewood water pails outhouses
boardwalks snares outboard motors chainsaws a church a schoolhouse the just-
completed community hall.

What are we tethered to when everything seems to collapse simultaneously?

The markings that we know are upended.

Collapse has a longer mark   an enduring seismic wave   in our memories.

The Good Friday Earthquake also called the Great Alaska Earthquake of March 27
1964 was the most powerful earthquake in US history. The magnitude 9.2
earthquake resulted in 131 deaths and was centred in Prince William Sound.

At 5:36 p.m. Alaska Standard Time a fault between the Pacific and North American Plates
ruptured near College Fjord in Prince William Sound. The earthquake lasted
four minutes
in most areas. Ocean floor shifts created large tsunamis. Vertical displacement of
up to 38 feet occurred, affecting an area of 100,000 miles^2 within Alaska.

Downtown Anchorage was heavily damaged and parts of the city built on clay
or near bluff, most notably the Turnagain Heights neighbourhood, suffered landslide
damage.

Most towns in the Prince William Sound Kenai Peninsula and Kodiak Island areas
especially the major ports of Seward and Kodiak were heavily hit by a combination of
seismic damage tsunamis subsidence fire.

Several of the smaller, low-lying Alaska Native villages in the area
Chenega and Afognak
were mostly or totally destroyed.

Perry Mead was a neurosurgeon in Anchorage who lost his two children in the
Great Alaska Earthquake at 5:36 p.m. on Good Friday 1964.

The Anchorage Daily News tells and re-tells this story fifty years later
alongside the stories of children whose parents were at the salon near the new
JC Penney store on Fifth Avenue in Anchorage. These stories are turned
over in our minds. They become the stories we remember because they
are written pressed circulated in varying degrees of honesty. In one story
Perry Mead's oldest son was a hero and rescued the toddler boy. In another
the daughter remembers her oldest brother dragged both boys out of the house
and threw them forward. Then in terror ran back into a house that collapsed
and was swallowed. This becomes a history.

Collapse has a longer mark   an enduring seismic wave   in our memories.

Determined by the river

We are thinking of a vessel that moves, that moves us and is moved.

We are thinking of a vessel and a movement at the pace of a river.

We are not concerned with a destination. We only know that we will be floating, skimming above, and moving at a speed determined by the river. We are moving.

We are building. We are building an impermanent structure. We are building something provisional within the gallery, a raft, a vessel. This structure is becoming. And we are floating. It is becoming a temporary structure to carry or hold Indigenous ideas, histories, objects, and forms – artworks from the collection of the Remai Modern configured in relation to one another and to artworks that we make. These works collectively are held by the vessel. We are floating above the museum, skimming the museum's surfaces.

We are speaking and listening to a geography, the South Saskatchewan River, a river that carves the grasses and rolling hills of the Saskatchewan prairies. A gathering place and catalyst for movement allowing Indigenous peoples to traverse the land via water-ways for a millenium, when we consider the South Saskatchewan River, we imagine Indigenous presences in the past, in the now and into the future – a continuance. How are – and how could – these continuous presences be activated?

When we consider an accumulation of time, we acknowledge the painful histories and current conditions of colonialism within Canada. We also consider and remember the significance of Indigenous knowledges that are rooted in place and shape our present.

We have gathered the work of sculptors, printmakers, painters, and photographers to be in relation to one another in *Determined by the river*. We are honoured to think alongside their work – Laurent Aksadjuak, Kenojuak Ashevak, Lori Blondeau, Bob Boyer, Ruth Cuthand, Robert James Houle, William Noah, Daphne Odjig, Jessie Oonark, Pudlo Pudlat, Allen Sapp, George Tataniq, Eli Tikeayak, Irene Avaalaaqiaq Tiktaalaaq, and two works by unknown Inuit artists.

We are gathering. Alongside the raft, we are gathering for conversations with Indigenous artists and thinkers to activate the exhibition with Indigenous ideas about artmaking, collections, and responsibilities to communities. These conversations will centre our collective concerns at this moment, which may be political and/or felt in our everyday lives. The participants are from Saskatchewan and Alberta. They have generously agreed to be with us, to speak. Collectively, we hope that our analysis will catalyze the museum and what it represents to act in accordance with history, in this moment, for the future. What does it mean for Indigenous people to be in relation to museums? What does it mean for museums to be in relation to Indigenous peoples? Participants in *Determined by the river: a discursive event* include Joi T. Arcand, Billy-Ray Belcourt, Lori Blondeau, Tasha Hubbard, Elwood Jimmy, and Erica Violet Lee.

i fall into this place between body and song

i wanted to begin in the place we are and how else to begin in Anishnaabeg territory than to begin through the making of a relationship with an Anishnaabekwe to begin with a woman who thinks through this land and with this land and in relation to this land i call the names of the women here Leanne Betasamosake Simpson Layli Long Soldier Cris Derksen Tanya Lukin Linklater

i call our names because there is something significant to this calling because erasure is palpable and ongoing and yet we continue we insist so i call you and i call on you to be here

and i wonder if this action is about many of us coming into this place – this structure – that on Anishnaabeg land and is a kind of structure akin perhaps to a museum and museums have been actively engaged in erasure of Indigenous peoples by treating us like we are remnants – our bodies, remnants – our ideas, remnants – our material objects, remnants

instead of remnants Leanne calls for repatriation she sings repatriation sings us back and Cris, her cello sings us back and in this singing we remember we remember that we are not remnants we reject the idea that we were ever remnants and that our ideas were ever remnants this is a generous act, an act of continuance

an Anishnaabekwe spoke publicly not long ago in northern Ontario – she spoke, she said that kandasowin is not separate from the people, the knowledge is not separate from the people our knowledges are embodied we sing our knowledges we sing to one another i sing to you now i sing in my drawings that are poems abstracted into constellations i sing to you in the wool duffle that wraps the table i sing to you in other ways i sing to you i sing to you i sing to you in this moment – in a text that only came to life because of this song

this is a generous act and in this generosity i simultaneously resist with an incisiveness at times because to endure we must persist and insist and resist and when i call you i know that you bring others with you we bring Anishnaabeg and Oglala Lakota and Cree and Alutiiq ones with us

i wonder if they want to be in this space with us and if they hear this song we sing that Leanne sings sings to barefeet and skin and spine and fingers and eyes and canoe bodies her and her and her shoulders and lake and sinks and seven stones and lake and suspend and sing and surrender and again and again and again and surrender and resist and drown and tread water and float and fall and surrender again and resist and fall and i think of all that is held within our bodies and inside of our songs and i fall into a place that is between body and song canoe bodies and cello bodies and this song i sing is one song of many lake songs canoe songs songs for stars songs for everyday and songs for love and life and songs to endure songs to barefeet and skin and spine and fingers and eyes and canoe bodies her and her and her shoulders and lake and sinks and seven stones and lake and suspend and in this place we are this feeling

the manoomin and berries and the man who used his own hands to make this food for all of us and i am grateful i am grateful for all of the people who work in this way who labour in this way the labour of harvesting the labour of tanning hide the labour of honouring the water and making songs the labour is a kind of continuance and i am labouring now and we are labouring to make space for others we labour not only for ourselves we labour for a future we insist

Notes

Gwi cuumillatstun. Uswillranka kingumni. I am like my Ancestors. My children are after me.

In 2005 I received support from Elders and Alutiiq language teachers the late Nick Alokli, the late Sophie Katelnikoff Shepherd, and Florence Pestrikoff. This was facilitated by April Laktonen Counceller at the Alutiiq Museum. The Elders translated songs I had composed into Sugcestun. I taught these songs to thirty Alutiiq youth in one of several youth culture camps organized by the Native Village of Afognak. The commitment and efforts to revitalize Sugcestun by these Elders are felt by the generations after them.

"Not Like Us" and "A girl"

These poems were written in November and December 2012 in response to the attempted assassination of girls' education activist Malala Yousafzai in the Swat Valley, Pakistan. These poems were written during a mentorship in poetry with Layli Long Soldier. Excerpts have been published elsewhere and performed and installed in galleries in Canada and the United States.

"44 days" and "The Harvest Sturdies"

These poems were written in the winter of 2012–2013 in response to Chief Theresa Spence's hunger strike, a forty-four-day action that began December 11, 2012. She fasted for treaty in a tipi on Victoria Island in the Ottawa River not far from Parliament Hill, Ottawa, Canada. The mitts Chief Spence wore in many of her press engagements may be understood as a symbol for the people of James Bay. Interviews with Agnes Hunter, Marlene Kapashesit, and Lillian Mishi Trapper in January and February 2013 supported the development of this poem. Their discussions of making traditional James Bay mitts are cited through direct quotations. "The Harvest Sturdies" was written during a mentorship in poetry with Layli Long Soldier. Excerpts have been published elsewhere and performed and installed in galleries and museums in Canada, the United States, and Europe.

Agnes Hunter and Duane Linklater provided spelling and translation of Cree words in "The Harvest Sturdies."
askiy: earth
astisak: mitts or mittens
atik: caribou
atikowayan: caribou hide
awasisak: children
iskwewak: women
napewak: men
nohkom: grandmother
nohkominanak: grandmothers
maskasina: moccasins

Editor Michael Nardone and I discussed my choice to include Cree translation in the book's notes rather than in close proximity to the poem. Encountering Cree language privileges Indigenous language as a way to enter, or to be refused access to, Indigenous thinking. Indigenous peoples continue to work to recover Indigenous languages as a result of colonial projects such as Indian Residential Schools, a system that actively worked to dismantle Indigenous languages, families, and our relationships to the Land. Indigenous peoples have historically experienced a range of emotions in relation to English language. At the very least, we can describe this experience as discomfort and not knowing. In the glossary I cite Cree speakers whom I describe as intergenerational language learners and teachers that I am in relation to.

"Event Score for Writing on Indigenous Contemporary Art (Mary Anne Barkhouse) 1–3"
Lukin Linklater, Tanya. "Video Documentation of *The Interlopers*, an Exhibition by
    Mary Anne Barkhouse." July 28, 2018. Video. MacLaren Art Centre, Barrie, ON.

Barkhouse, Mary Anne. *Midden (Au Grand Couvert)*. 2018, ongoing. Installation.
    MacLaren Art Centre, Barrie, ON.

--. Untitled I–VIII from *The Quick and the Dead*. 2018, ongoing. Anthotypes and cyanotypes. MacLaren Art Centre, Barrie, ON.

"Visiting"
Barkhouse, Mary Anne. Personal communication. August 13, 2018.

"On tables"
A similar question was posed by Mary Anne Barkhouse during our telephone conversation on August 13, 2018.

"For midden found by Mary Anne Barkhouse near her home on the side of the road and cast in porcelain by her hands"
Oxford English Dictionary. 3rd ed. (online). S.v. "midden, n." Accessed August 2018. www.oed.com/view/Entry/118135.
Simpson, Leanne Betasamosake. "Nishnaabeg Resurgence: Stories from Within" and "Theorizing Resurgence from within Nishnaabeg Thought." In *Dancing on Our Turtle's Back: Stories of Nishnaabeg Re-Creation, Resurgence and a New Emergence*, 11–48. Winnipeg: Arbeiter Ring Publishing (ARP Books), 2011.

Within an Alaskan context, the Great Death refers to the 1918 Spanish flu epidemic that devastated families and villages across the state. I consider the Great Death durational for Alutiit extending to the devastating event, Refuge Rock, on Kodiak Island in the 1780s and continuing to the Spanish flu epidemic of 1918.

"In Memoriam/Unspoken–ness"
Originally titled "In Memoriam," this version of the poem reflects its subsequent titling for exhibition, *Unspoken–ness*. The poem refers to a dark period in Alutiiq history during imperial rule with Russian fur traders' violent management of Alutiit and our lands, as well as an event, Refuge Rock, which broke Alutiiq resistance. Our people continue to deal with the effects of intergenerational grief resulting from this event and our subsequent enslavement.

I composed this poem in 2011, referencing *A Conversational Dictionary of Kodiak Alutiiq*, compiled by Jeff Leer and published in 1978 by the Alaska Native Language Centre at University of Alaska Fairbanks. I have not included translation in past publication and exhibition of the poem maintaining that Indigenous languages do not require translation for a reader. In this way, I gesture towards my complex relationship to Sugcestun, Alutiiq language, my mother tongue. For this book, I chose to re-find the translations. Because the dictionary only provides the translation from English to Alutiiq and I relied on memory to locate words, I could not find the translation for *esgarluni*. I changed the word to *ellpeklluku*, meaning to sense it.

elltuwaq: grandchild
ellpeklluku: sense it
niicugniluku: listen to it, for it
tangerlluku: see it
tengluni: fly, take off

"Decommission"
This text was written for the catalogue accompanying Duane Linklater's 2013 exhibition *Decommission* at the MacLaren Art Centre in Barrie, Ontario.

"An Event Score for Kodiak Alutiit 1 (Helen Simeonoff)"
Kari Cwynar, in a Skype conversation on March 12, 2016, described my practice as "sparse and melancholic."

"They fall the ground beneath you"
Written in 2016, this text later became a part of a video installation. Sonya Kelliher-Combs is committed to process, memory, community, and embodied practices, and her practice has carved space for Alaska Native peoples' concerns. The video installation is in relation to Afognak, family, embodied knowledges, trauma, and memory, and features Mina Linklater, Sassa Linklater, Tanya Lukin Linklater, Tessa Pizzale, and Keisha Stone. A performance, *Untitled (for Sonya Kelliher-Combs)*, took place in relation to Sonya Kelliher-Combs's *Orange Curl*, 2012 at Crystal Bridges Museum of American Art for the exhibition, *Art for a New Understanding, Native Voices, 1950s to Now*. After seven days of open rehearsals, a series of performances occurred with dancers Ceinwen Gobert and Hanako Hoshimi-Caines.

I have heavily appropriated text for sections of this poem. Accounts of the Good Friday Earthquake were gathered from the Native Village of Afognak website, the Anchorage Daily News, as well as in stories held and told by my relatives to me over the years (www .afognak.org). In parts of the poem I have italicized quotations from these respective sources or summarized the stories that they tell.

I have appropriated sections of text from the Alaska Pacific Emergency Preparedness Net, "one of the oldest emergency traffic handling nets on amateur radio. The net originated in 1964 during the aftermath of the Alaska earthquake known as the Good Friday Earthquake...During that disaster government and private communication systems failed, and Ham radio operators provided vital links to the rest of the world." www.alaskapacificnet.org.

"Determined by the river"
This text was written in collaboration with Duane Linklater for an exhibition, *Determined by the river*, in 2017 for the opening of the museum, Remai Modern, in Saskatoon. The text was also published in the catalogue, *Field Guide*, to accompany the inaugural exhibition of the Remai Modern.

"i fall into this place between body and song"
This text was written in twenty-eight minutes during Leanne Betasamosake Simpson's performance of "How to Steal a Canoe" accompanied by Cris Derksen at Artspace Peterborough in September 2016. Leanne performed the poem seven times. I performed this newly written text after their performance. The text lives in a state of unfinishedness, in process, as a becoming that lives through performance.

The phrase "the knowledge is not separate from the people" is my memory of a presentation at the Anishnaabewin 7 Conference, "Voices of the Land, Voices of the Ether," organized by the Ojibwe Cultural Foundation in Sudbury, Ontario, in March 2016.

Acknowledgments

This book was written in small doses between 2011 and 2017. I am grateful for Layli Long Soldier's incisive writing, generosity, editing, conversation, and mentorship in Indigenous poetry and poetics. Dylan Robinson's encouragement and space for me to write in unconventional critical and literary ways in his graduate courses facilitated several of these works. Michael Nardone, editor, took an interest in my work several years ago at an exhibition. He believed in a book to be, and this publication could not have happened without his belief. Agnes Hunter, Marlene Kapashesit, and Lillian Mishi Trapper agreed to be interviewed about their experiences and knowledge of sewing, beading, and tanning hides. Without their agreement, "The Harvest Sturdies" and other poems, or several subsequent years of artistic production, would not have come into being. I am grateful to Magdalyn Asimakis who sought out my writing on numerous occasions for publication and exhibition and for other curators who were compelled by my writing practice. Ivan Lukin's enduring support culminated in him telling me that I should write a book for our people. Quyanaasinaq, mîkwec to Nione Boydstun, Sarah Lukin, Shauna Hegna, the late Pauline Linklater, Lauree Linklater Pizzale, and Cynthia Cowan for kindness, honesty, laughter, strength, and love. I am grateful for Duane Linklater's support. Our continued conversation and collaboration have been significant for my thinking. I hope that this book might help our children, Mina, Tobi, and Sassa, remember what it means to be Alutiiq and to imagine. Indeed, while they are my primary audience, I also write for my community of Alutiit and for Indigenous youth.

With thanks for the support of the Ontario Arts Council for a mentorship in poetry with Layli Long Soldier and a grant for the production of writing.

A number of these works have been previously published, performed, or shown in exhibition. Publications (including excerpts) are noted below.

Lukin Linklater, Tanya. "Excerpts from 'A glossary of insistence.'" In *The Routledge Companion of Indigenous Art Histories in Canada and the United States*, edited by Heather Igloliorte and Carla Taunton, chap. 34. Routledge Art History and Visual Studies Companions series. London: Routledge, 2023.

––. "The Harvest Sturdies." In *Ndè Sìi Wet'aʔà: Northern Indigenous Voices on Land, Life, & Art*, edited by Kyla LeSage, Thumlee Drybones-Foliot, and Leanne Betasamosake Simpson. Winnipeg: ARP, 2022.

––. The Interlopers*, an Exhibition by Mary Anne Barkhouse*. Barrie, ON: MacLaren Art Centre, 2018. maclarenart.com/wp-content/uploads/2018/11/The-Interlopers_Gallery-Handout.pdf. Exhibition catalogue.

––. "Not Like Us." *níchiwamiskwém | nimidet | my sister | ma sœur*. La Biennale d'art contemporain autochtone (BACA), 4th ed., May 4 to June 16, 2018. La GGuilde, Tiohtià:ke / Mooniyaang / Montréal, QC.

––. "Event Scores." 2018. *13 Ways to Summon Ghosts*, May 16 to September 1, 2018. Gordon Smith Gallery of Canadian Art, North Vancouver, BC.

––. "Nohkom," "44," and "A girl." *Slay All Day*, September 21 to October 15, 2018. ma ma gallery, Toronto, ON.

––. "i fall into a place that is between body and song." In *ALMANAC*, edited by Maggie Groat. Kitchener, ON: Kitchener-Waterloo Art Gallery, 2017.

––. "Selection of Event Scores." In *That I am looking backwards and into for a purpose, to go on: A Companion Publication*, edited by Magdalyn Asimakis, Jared Quinton, and Alexandra Symons Sutcliffe. New York: Independent Study Program of the Whitney Museum of American Art, 2017.

––. "An Event Score for Maria Tallchief, Dylan Robinson and Sherry Farrell Racette," "An Event Score for Kodiak Alutiit 1 (Helen Simeonoff)," and "An Event Score for Kodiak Alutiit 2 (To Aleš Hrdlička)." In *A Parallel Excavation: Duane Linklater and Tanya Lukin Linklater*, with writing by Tiffany Shaw-Collinge, Duane Linklater, Tanya Lukin Linklater, and Erin Sutherland. Edmonton: Art Gallery of Alberta, 2016. Exhibition catalogue.

––. "Nohkom" and "44." *First American Art Magazine* 10 (Spring 2016): 38–47. firstamericanartmagazine.com/faam10_spring2016/.

––. "A girl" and "Not Like Us." *Yellow Medicine Review: A Journal of Indigenous Literature, Art and Thought* (Spring 2015). Guest-edited by Joan Kane. www.yellowmedicinereviewstore.com/store/p5/Yellow_Medicine_Review%2C_Spring_2015_Issue.html.

––. "The Harvest Sturdies (Excerpts)." *Taos International Journal of Poetry and Art* (2014). Edited by Veronica Golos. www.taosjournalofpoetry.com/the-harvest-sturdies-excerpts/.

––. "Untitled." *As Us* 4. Special issue, "Decolonial Love." Guest-edited by Tria Andrews, Carlos Contreras, Diahndra Grill, Casandra Lopez, and Tanaya Winder. asusjournal.org/issue-4/tanya-lukin-linklater-poetry/.

––. "Decommission." In *Duane Linklater's Decommission*, MacLaren Art Centre, Barrie, ON, 2013. maclarenart.com/wp-content/uploads/2018/02/DLinklater_Decommission-brochure_Final.pdf. Exhibition catalogue.

––. "In Memoriam." *Drunken Boat* 12. Special folio, "Native American Women's Poetry." Guest-edited by Layli Long Soldier. d7.drunkenboat.com/db15/tanya-lukin-linklater.html.

Lukin Linklater, Tanya, with Andrew Berardini. "An Event Score for Afognak Alutiit 1–4," "An Event Score for Haunting (Eve Tuck)," and "An Event Score for the Epistemic Violence of Translation (Edgar Heap of Birds)." *Mousse Magazine* 54 (Summer 2016).

Lukin Linklater, Tanya, and Duane Linklater. *Determined by the river*. October 21 to January 7, 2017. Exhibition. Remai Modern, Saskatoon, SK.

Works Cited

Alaska-Pacific Emergency Preparedness Net (website). Edited by Larry Nudson. Accessed March 16, 2016. alaskapacificnet.org.

Barkhouse, Mary Anne. Personal communication. August 13, 2018.

––. *Midden (Au Grand Couvert)*. 2018, ongoing. Installation. MacLaren Art Centre, Barrie, ON.

––. Untitled I–VIII from *The Quick and the Dead*. 2018, ongoing. Anthotypes and cyanotypes. MacLaren Art Centre, Barrie, ON.

Kalmus, Peter. "The Best Medicine for My Climate Grief." *YES!*, August 9, 2018. www.yesmagazine.org/mental-health/the-best-medicine-for-my-climate -grief-20180809.

Kelliher-Combs, Sonya. *Orange Curl*. 2012. Sculpture. Crystal Bridges Museum of American Art, Bentonville, AR.

Linklater, Duane. *Decommission*. December 5 to March 9, 2014. Exhibition. MacLaren Art Centre, Barrie, ON.

Lukin, Ivan. Personal communication. 1993–2018.

Lukin Linklater, Tanya. *They fall the ground beneath you*. 2018. Work for camera. Crystal Bridges Museum of American Art, Bentonville, AR.

––. *Untitled (for Sonya Kelliher-Combs)*. 2018. Performance. Crystal Bridges Museum of American Art, Bentonville, AR.

––. "Video Documentation of *The Interlopers*, an Exhibition by Mary Anne Barkhouse." July 28, 2018. Video. MacLaren Art Centre, Barrie, ON.

Lukin Linklater, Tanya, and Duane Linklater. *Determined by the river*. October 21 to January 7, 2017. Exhibition. Remai Modern, Saskatoon, SK.

Native Village of Afognak. "Oral History Archive." Accessed 2016 and 2019. www.afognak.org/oral-history-archive/.

The Nature of Things. Season 52, episode 10, "Meet the Coywolf." Directed by Susan
  Fleming. Written by Siobhan Flanagan and Gary Lang. Starring Stan Gehrt,
  Erich Muntz, and Nora Young. Aired February 14, 2013, on CBC.

O'Malley, Julia. "March 27, 1964: The Day the Earth Fell to Pieces for One
  Anchorage Family." *Anchorage Daily News*, March 22, 2014, updated
  December 10, 2018. www.adn.com/our-alaska/article/march-27-1964-day
  -earth-fell-pieces-one-anchorage-family/2014/03/23/.

Oxford English Dictionary. 3rd ed. (online). S.v. "midden, *n*." Accessed August 2018.
  www.oed.com/view/Entry/118135.

Simpson, Leanne Betasamosake. "Nishnaabeg Resurgence: Stories from Within" and
  "Theorizing Resurgence from within Nishnaabeg Thought." In *Dancing on Our
  Turtle's Back: Stories of Nishnaabeg Re-Creation, Resurgence and a New Emergence*,
  11–48. Winnipeg: Arbeiter Ring Publishing (ARP Books), 2011.

Simpson, Leanne Betasamosake, with Cris Derksen. "How to Steal a Canoe."
  September 16, 2016. Performance. Artspace Peterborough, Peterborough, ON.

Documenting Physical Investigations with Language

A dialogue with Tanya Lukin Linklater (2020)

Michael Nardone

When I first encountered your writings, it was in a visual arts context: you had printed excerpts from your poem sequence "The Harvest Sturdies" on canvas tarps that were installed throughout Open Space, the artist-run centre in Victoria, British Columbia. Close to the works were stunning videos of these tarp-texts also installed out on the land, in northern Ontario. Can you discuss the journey of these texts towards *Slow Scrape*, your writing of them, and the various forms of their publication prior to this book?

Tanya Lukin Linkater

I hadn't intended on writing a book. I worked on each of these texts at different times within different contexts from 2011 to 2017. The poem "In Memoriam" was written in 2011 and was published in a special issue of *Drunken Boat* guest edited by Layli Long Soldier. I had met Layli at Bard College where she was studying and I was visiting one summer. "In Memoriam" is a text in relation to a series of works: performances and video I had developed during that time centred on specific histories on my island that were violent and resulted in intergenerational grief, displacement, and loss of language and Alutiiq ways of being. I was interested partly in the ways in which memory lives in the body beyond an event or a series of events and possibly how it manifests for generations. I suppose I was also interested in how we make sense of ourselves in this time, given the constraints of history that have produced our current context. I considered text as part of a larger process of this investigation of history, memory, and the body. I later asked Layli if she was open to a poetry mentorship in 2012–2013. We met weekly or bi-weekly via Skype. I lived on Nipissing First Nation in northern Ontario at the time and she lived in Tsaile, Arizona. Across that distance, we read together. She encouraged me to write about what felt urgent.

There were political actions taking place that were very present for me as I watched them unfold on social media that fall and winter: Chief Theresa Spence's hunger strike, Idle No More, and round dance actions in shopping malls at Christmas time in Canada. I was also moved by the attempted assassination of Malala Yousafzi, a girls' education activist, which I read partly in relation to discourses surrounding education within a Canadian context of the legacy of Indian Residential Schools and the Truth and Reconciliation Commission of Canada. I wrote "Not like us," "The Harvest Sturdies," and "A girl" during this mentorship as I worked through some of my thinking around education, treaty, and women's experiences and work in relation to both.

It was an intensive research process. I interviewed three of my Omaskeko Cree relatives for "The Harvest Sturdies," asking them about their lives. I wasn't exactly certain what I was asking them. As the interviews unfolded, it became clear that my request extended to a remembering of relations – of family and with the land in ways I could not have anticipated. They also shared about the very private cultivation of their inner lives. These works were a form of documentary poetics in that I directly quote my relatives. I wanted to reflect their generosity and concision in the writing, and this was in alignment with a way of writing that I developed over this time.

What is the relationship between these compositions and your visual arts practice?

I often attempt to make sense of the world through writing. Years ago during a studio visit, Pablo de Ocampo described writing as the substrate of my arts practice.

Occasionally, I install text works in museums or galleries. In "The Harvest Sturdies," I've used visual poetry to reference a stretched hide, the repetition of beadwork, or smoke in a tipi that is colouring the hide. For this project I chose to print on canvas or tarp-like material that we might use for a tipi or a temporary shelter on the land, citing the home and the land as the locations for intergenerational learning that Agnes Hunter, Marlene Kapashesit, and Lillian Trapper shared with me.

I've started bringing text into my video work in more pronounced ways in the last couple of years. I began to make text works, videos, and sculptures for exhibition partly as a way for the work to travel without me, to circulate beyond the live event. I was concerned that if my work only lived in performance, it might disappear or be erased. As an Alaska Native woman I think about the history of discourse surrounding Native Americans in the United States – the ongoing trope of the vanishing Indian as well as the substantive efforts to erase our intellectual traditions, to marginalize our contributions to most fields: an epistemic violence. The live event, even the exhibition, disappears. Perhaps my practice shouldn't be remembered; others have to decide that. But moving towards the art object in small ways means that my work can have a life that extends into the future.

I've often thought about how contemporary dance is an abstract form. My videos, attentive to the body, communities, architecture, or landscape, might also be considered abstract for an everyday viewer to encounter in the museum. I consider text as a potential way for the viewer to enter into the work; however, I balance this access with strategies of refusal.

In situating the texts within your visual arts practice, perhaps I overemphasize the object itself, which is something you are of course interested in, but, with that, throughout your work, there is, like you say, a refusal of that by means of a different emphasis on the live event, in movement, in choreography. So I'm curious if you could also discuss the relationship between your writings and this other element that is central to your work?

I am perhaps most known for making performances or videos with dancers. An older Anishnaabe man where I live (the small city of

North Bay, Ontario) recently told me that I make things *happen*. That was a significant comment, as it was a recognition by a community member of the live event, of the ways in which I labour to make an event happen. It's a kind of slow build over time that becomes visible in performance but takes ongoing daily investigations, reflection, reading, thinking, conversations with curators, etc. Writing is an important part of this process. It documents these moments. These are processes dependent upon a number of constraints or conditions that I've put into place and require a flexible responsiveness. So much of my practice is in relation and in response to histories, to the present moment, to the conditions of the museum, to the conversations I'm having with dancers, composers, curators, etc.

At times, I document physical investigations with language, distilling language from conversation with dancers. The dancers and I notate their dances in different ways. I keep my notes for future investigations or performances, building over time. It can be a kind of back and forth between languages, possibly a kind of continuous translation between the body (which comes to have its own series of languages initiated by the dancer), materials (including cultural belongings made by our Ancestors), and other forms. I tend to jot down key questions in journals that I later ask during the choreographic process. Or I document questions that come up during the performance-making process through conversation or connections I am thinking through. Often writing is a very unseen part of my practice. This writing may never be shared publicly. I consider my journal to be a working space, a studio of sorts.

In terms of the ways in which poems and event scores are visibly or audibly present in my practice, since 2013 I've been reading texts alongside dancers and/or my videos. I have allowed myself the space for these performances with dancers to fail; I consider them to be studies, experiments. In some cases, the poems are a score, structure or script for the making of a dance within the museum or gallery. I work through an open rehearsal process to build these performances and have come to work with a group of five independent dancers, each of whom have different strengths, movement languages, and views that they bring to the process.

The readings with videos are configured differently each time: I choose different poems, event scores, and videos for each event. I'm particularly interested in moments where my voice collides with the image in a way that may never happen again. I can't fully anticipate these moments. I leave that to chance and give myself the constraint of thirty minutes of video and thirty minutes of text. I time the performance at the live event but don't rehearse in advance. This means that the readings or interpretations of both the poems and videos might be infinite.

I see throughout *Slow Scrape* a movement between action ("making things happen") and a memory (documentation), both thematically and formally in the design of the texts. I'd love to focus on the latter for a moment – memory, with all of its partialities, scars, gaps, richnesses, the ways of being these poems are constantly imagining and articulating, their possible futures and assembly of relations. Can you discuss how forms of memory materialize and are materialized within these writings?

I don't think I'm unlike many Indigenous peoples in this commitment to remembering and continuous action. The idea that I make things *happen* reminded me that the liveness of the event in this moment is a part of a durational inheritance that extends to my Ancestors. What I mean to say is that making things happen, organizing large scale events for families and communities was and continues to be an Alutiiq practice.

My work continuously considers orality, embodiment, our philosophical concerns, history, and the present moment. I wonder broadly about how we have continued to insist on our Indigeneity (Alutiiq-ness or Sugpiaq-ness in my case) in the face of dominant systems that have actively dismantled our languages, minds, and relationships to ourselves. I'm interested partly in memory embodied at the scale of felt structures that insist in the midst of the historical. Elsewhere, I've begun to write about insistence as an accumulation of quotidian, minor actions that in some moments become visible. I think my larger practice investigates the ways in which the relational, coded in orality (including embodiment) and connected to the material, allows for this insistence. This insistence is not only concerned with the past but allows for our peoples' ways of being and knowing in the present towards a continuance, our future, where possible.

My thinking is in alignment with discourses initiated in the late 1960s by Indigenous peoples – practitioners and theorists working in relation to their communities, to sovereignty, to justice, and to what has come to be described as resurgence – that continue today. I situate my practice within these larger histories, yet I'm speaking from specific moments and experiences that I've encountered in my lifetime or that I've come to know about. I feel a deep responsibility to our Ancestors, to today, and to the future. I think that the real work is happening in communities – in my villages and across Alaska, in Nbisiing Anishnaabeg territory where I live, in Cree communities in Canada that I am in relation to as well. My artistic practice and writing gesture towards that.

When I first read your event scores, I immediately thought of them as reformulating Fluxus and other historical avant-garde practices in a newly engaged way. Here, I think of people like Allan Kaprow, George Brecht, Yoko Ono, among others. Were you drawing from this tradition, or, if not, were there other artists or aesthetic tendencies that animated the possibility of these works for you?

The event scores arose out of a graduate course with Dylan Robinson called "Indigenous & Settler Affect: Unsettling~Writing~Feeling" at Queen's University in the spring of 2016. Dylan shared a series of event scores with us and we were encouraged to write in a range of ways. I was particularly moved by Yoko Ono's event scores. I also experienced what I perceived to be a live event score when Eber Hampton led an Indigenous conference delegation at the University of Alberta through verbal directions for a small series of physical actions that were intended to slow our sense of time and connect us to our breath as a greeting of the sun. This small action was quite profound for me within that context as it was unexpected. Even though I had experienced these kinds of directions within dance and performance studio classes over decades and have also led these kinds of exercises in various spaces, it was quite striking to listen, breathe, visualize, and move within this other space. It helped to create a shared experience among the group.

I found it quite easy to rest into this way of writing. It was generative to me in its concision (which is a form of refusal), the almost plain language, and its intentionality.

I connected this idea directly to my experience of performance. Yet I also considered that the event score could function solely as a text. I have performed the event scores at times, but not as a set of directions for an audience; instead as a distilled, concise text that I've spoken, sometimes accompanied by video. A number of works in this book were written initially for that course and went on to be published, performed, or integrated into video works later.

Another element that stands out for me in *Slow Scrape* is the practices of listening that are at its core – something that is deeply allied with my own interests in poetry and artistic practices. And perhaps, in the frame of listening, this is where memory and action come together in a fruitful way. I can see a few different forms of listening that take place throughout this work: intergenerational listening, translinguistic listening (Alutiiq, Cree, English), mediated listening (through global and national news, and also through one's personal relations), terrestrial or land-based listening (topological). Are there other forms that you see? Can you discuss if or how these forms of listening inform your practices?

I appreciate your analysis across these different contexts. Mostly I consider that listening is an integral part of being Indigenous. My early training in listening came as a youth at the kitchen table where my dad visited with aunties, uncles, and other relatives, neighbours, and community members. He also spent considerable time with my sisters and me on the land and waters near my village hunting and fishing. I have not attained my father's ability to discern weather, the tides, or the messages left by animals, birds, and fish at home. This discernment takes a lifetime of experience, and I left my village as a young person to attend university. Yet this early training, listening to relatives visit or my father teach us about gillnetting salmon and when the different species run annually allowed me to later spend time with Anishnaabe and Cree Elders and knowledge holders in Alberta as a young adult, listening, attuning myself to their way of speaking and communicating. This time in Alberta within these invisible networks was quite formative for me. I've continued this practice of listening in my adult life. Listening is connected to learning, which means synthesizing knowledge – integrating ideas into what we already know or upending what we think we know in order to apply that knowledge to our lives, to change our practices, a process that may take years. However it also means that when we listen, we learn a level of discernment and responsibility in this listening. I might also mention that I listen to the voice, to conversation, to sound, to the body, to the multiple ways we communicate in everyday life and in the performances I organize. This listening is multi-sensorial. Elwood Jimmy speaks about an enlivened and expanded listening; I think a great deal about listening with the full body.

In reading through the book, I wonder if part of this listening practice is situated within a concept of mentorship, in intentional acts of accumulating and transmitting cultural knowledge? Perhaps "mentorship" isn't the right word, but what I mean to gesture towards are the thoughtful ways you foreground your relations with others, which is both an acknowledgment of indebtedness as well as a commitment to give back.

I look to people in my life who have provided moments of guidance over time. Our grandmother in Peawanuck, Agnes Hunter, my late auntie, Sue Lukin, aunties Marlene Kapashesit and Irene Iserhoff Linklater, my late mother-in-law, Pauline Linklater, and my father, Ivan Lukin, have shared their life experiences with me. I look to the work of artists, writers, and thinkers who came before me, learning from their cultural production. A few of these are Rebecca Belmore, Marilyn Dumont, Joy Harjo, Sonya Kelliher-Combs, Ralph Lemon, Rita Letendre, Senga Nengudi, Karen Pheasant, Rosy Simas, and Maria Tallchief. I look to cultural belongings found in museum collections as information or instructions left by my Ancestors. Often I connect with my peers and we learn from one another. Here I consider Raven Chacon, Candice Hopkins, Heather Igloliorte, Elwood Jimmy, Duane Linklater, Layli Long Soldier, Julie Nagam, Laura Ortman, Karyn Recollet, Wendy Red Star, and Jennifer Wabano. I learn from my children, from the Anishnaabeg and Cree youth in North Bay where I have lived for over a decade, and from other young relatives. Knowledge is not only transmitted from older generations to young people; the transmission of knowledge is multi-directional. I think of Ivanie Aubin-Malo's knowledge of contemporary and fancy shawl dance and Billy-Ray Belcourt's incisive writing. These young Indigenous folks teach me. Perhaps this book is something I am leaving for others. My artistic work does not tend to travel home to Alaska. It is my hope that this book can make it home.